Washington

Jim Ollhoff

Visit us at
www.abdopublishing.com

Published by ABDO Publishing Company, 8000 West 78th Street, Suite 310, Edina, Minnesota 55439 USA. Copyright ©2010 by Abdo Consulting Group, Inc. International copyrights reserved in all countries. No part of this book may be reproduced in any form without written permission from the publisher. The Checkerboard Library™ is a trademark and logo of ABDO Publishing Company.

Printed in the United States.

Editor: John Hamilton
Graphic Design: Sue Hamilton
Cover Illustration: Neil Klinepier
Cover Photo: iStock

Manufactured with paper
containing at least 10%
post-consumer waste

Interior Photo Credits: Alamy, AP Images, City of Tumwater, Comstock, Corbis, C.W. Peale, Fort Vancouver National Historic Site, Getty, Granger Collection, Independence National Historical Park, iStock Photo, Library of Congress, Mile High Maps, Mountain High Maps, One Mile Up, Peter Arnold, R. Schlect, Seattle Mariners, Seattle Seahawks, Seattle Sonics, Seattle Storm, Secretary of State-Washington, USGS/Cascades Volcano Observatory, and Wikimedia.

Statistics: State population statistics taken from 2008 U.S. Census Bureau estimates. City and town population statistics taken from July 1, 2007, U.S. Census Bureau estimates. Land and water area statistics taken from 2000 Census, U.S. Census Bureau.

Library of Congress Cataloging-in-Publication Data

Ollhoff, Jim, 1959-
   Washington / Jim Ollhoff.
       p. cm. -- (The United States)
   Includes index.
   ISBN 978-1-60453-683-6
   1. Washington (State)--Juvenile literature. I. Title.

F891.3.O54 2010
979.7--dc22
                                    2008052881

Table of Contents

The Evergreen State

The state of Washington is named after George Washington, the first president of the United States. Washington state has a little bit of everything. It has forests, mountains, deserts, and coastline. Washington has high technology, manufacturing, and farming. It has ultra-modern cities, and remote wilderness. It has mild weather in the west, and harsh weather in the east.

People from Washington love their state, especially people who love nature. It is heavily forested. Majestic mountains rise on the horizon. Many people think Washington is a great place to call home.

Built for the 1962 World's Fair, the Space Needle has become one of the most famous buildings in Seattle.

Quick Facts

Name: The state is named after George Washington, the first U.S. president.

State Capital: Olympia, population 44,925

Date of Statehood: November 11, 1889 (42nd state)

Population: 6,549,224 (13th-most populous state)

Area (Total Land and Water): 71,300 square miles (184,666 sq km), 18th-largest state

Largest City: Seattle, population 594,210

Nickname: The Evergreen State

Motto: *Alki* (Into the Future/By and By)

State Bird: Willow Goldfinch

State Flower: Coast Rhododendron

State Rock: Petrified Wood

State Tree: Western Hemlock

State Song: "Washington, My Home"

Highest Point: Mount Rainier, 14,410 feet (4,392 meters)

Lowest Point: Pacific Ocean, 0 feet (0 m)

Average July Temperature: 68°F (20°C)

Record High Temperature: 118°F (48°C) at Ice Harbor Dam on August 5, 1961

Average January Temperature: 34°F (1°C)

Record Low Temperature: -48°F (-44°C) at Mazama and Winthrop on December 30, 1968

Mount Rainier

Average Annual Precipitation: The Olympic Peninsula exceeds 135 inches (343 cm), but other places get less than 6 inches (15 cm)

Number of U.S. Senators: 2

Number of U.S. Representatives: 9

Pacific Ocean

U.S. Postal Service Abbreviation: WA

Geography

Washington is the 18th-largest state. Much of the western side of Washington is forest.

There are also many mountains in the western part of Washington. The biggest is Mount Rainier, in the Cascade Range. The Cascade Range is a line of tall mountains that runs north and south. Mount Rainier is 14,410 feet (4,392 m) above sea level. Many of the high mountains have glaciers near the top.

Mount St. Helens continues to be an active volcano today.

Washington has volcanoes, too. Mount St. Helens is 96 miles (154 km) south of Seattle. It erupted on May 18, 1980, causing a lot of damage and costing many lives.

Washington's total land and water area is 71,300 square miles (184,666 sq km). It is the 18th-largest state. The state capital is Olympia.

In the southeast corner of the state, the Blue Mountains rise up. They have gentle slopes, going up about 6,000 feet (1,829 m). Near the Blue Mountains there is a high plateau called the Columbia Plateau. There are few plants because it doesn't rain very much there. Stemming out from the plateau are deep, dry valleys. These are called coulees. They were cut by melting glacier water thousands of years ago.

The main rivers in Washington are the Columbia River, Snake River, and Yakima River. Major lakes include Lake Franklin D. Roosevelt and Lake Washington.

The western edge of Washington meets the Pacific Ocean. It is flat along the coast, so many businesses and homes are built there. There are many ocean inlets called sounds. Near Seattle, the ocean waterway is called Puget Sound. Its deep waters make Seattle a good harbor for ships.

About half of the people in Washington live in the area around Seattle. About one-fourth of the state's population lives in rural areas.

The Columbia River runs through Washington's Beacon Rock State Park. The Columbia River is one of the main rivers in Washington.

Climate and Weather

The Pacific Ocean makes the western side of Washington very mild. The ocean makes the summers cooler and the winters warmer. In Seattle, an average January temperature is 41 degrees Fahrenheit (5°C). The average July temperature in Seattle is 66 degrees Fahrenheit (19°C).

Along the coastal areas, there is a lot of rain. Near Seattle, it might rain 40 inches (102 cm) per year. Farther inland, it sometimes rains 100 inches (254 cm) per year.

The Cascade Range of mountains forms a wall that stops mild ocean weather. On the west side of the mountains, the ocean creates mild temperatures. On the east side of the mountains, there is a much bigger range of temperatures, and much less rainfall.

There is a lot of rain along the coast of Washington state. It can rain 100 inches (254 cm) per year.

Plants and Animals

Washington has more than 23 million acres (9.3 million ha) of forest, covering half of the state. Most of the forests are in the western side of the state. Common trees include Douglas fir, western red cedar, and ponderosa pine. The western hemlock is the official state tree.

In eastern Washington, common trees include western white pine, ponderosa pine, and the western larch.

The biggest animals in Washington are deer, elk, bears, pumas, and mountain goats. In the very western wilderness part of Washington, large herds of Olympic elk still roam. The Canada lynx, coyote, and red fox can also be found. Smaller animals, such as raccoons, beavers, skunks, minks, and otters can be found all over the state.

An elk grazes in Olympic National Park.

Black Bear

Otter

Raccoon

An orca, also known as a killer whale, is the largest member of the dolphin family.

Orcas and harbor seals make their home in the ocean along the coast. Pacific salmon leave the ocean and swim into the streams of Washington to spawn. Other common fish in Washington lakes and rivers include trout, largemouth and smallmouth bass, grayling, and white sturgeon.

Great Horned Owls live and hunt in the forests of Washington state.

Birds that live in Washington include crows, ravens, thrushes, Oregon jays, western tanagers, kingfishers, and ruffed grouse. The willow goldfinch, the state bird, is also found in the forests. Bald eagles, hawks, and owls hunt in the forests.

Inashah, a Yakima native.

A Yakima reed mat teepee.

People arrived in the Washington area about 10,000 to 15,000 years ago. They were hunters following herds of animals.

By the time the first Europeans came, there were many Native American tribes living in the area. Major tribes included the Chinook, Coast Salish, Nez Percé, and the Yakima.

Captain James Cook, the famous English explorer, is believed to be the first European to trade with Washington's Native Americans in the late 1770s.

In about 1775, Spanish explorer Bruno de Heceta sailed along the Washington coast. In 1778, English explorer Captain James Cook also sailed through the area. He was the first to trade with the Native Americans. In 1792, another English explorer, Captain George Vancouver, completed a detailed map of the coast and the inland waterways.

Explorers found that the pelts of sea otters and seals could be sold for much money in China and Europe. Fur traders from Spain, England, Russia, France, and the United States sent ships to the Washington coast.

Meriwether Lewis and William Clark.

In 1805, the Lewis and Clark Expedition reached Washington. They had traveled all the way overland from Missouri.

In the 1840s, settlers started coming to Washington by way of the Oregon Trail. This was a trail leading through Nebraska, Wyoming, and Idaho. By 1853, the area became a part of the United States called Washington Territory.

Washington officials offered land to settlers. Sadly, it was the land of the Native American tribes. Often, the land was given away without the knowledge of the tribes who lived there. Sometimes the relationships with the

Native Americans were peaceful. Sometimes there were bloody battles.

In the 1880s, railroads linked Washington with states in the East. The population surged. On November 11, 1889, Washington became the 42nd state. The first governor was Elisha Ferry.

In 1896, gold was discovered in northwest Canada's Yukon region. Seattle became a center for gold seekers on their way north.

A Seattle street in 1880.

A poster, created during World War I, promotes shipbuilding.

ON THE JOB FOR VICTORY
UNITED STATES SHIPPING BOARD   EMERGENCY FLEET CORPORATION

During World War I (1914-1918), Washington's economy boomed. The nation needed lumber from the forests, and a port to build ships. The war helped Washington's economy.

In the 1920s, Washington's economy worsened. Whole forests had been cut down, so it was harder to harvest lumber. Shipbuilding stopped after the war. The Great Depression, beginning in 1929, hit the state hard.

Historically, loggers cut down entire forests. This was known as clear-cutting.

During America's involvement in World War II (1941-1945), the economy improved. Shipbuilding became important again. Aircraft construction and atomic energy projects helped the state. The population surged again.

After the war, Washington became the center of many industries. Working with metals, building jet planes, and shipbuilding were continued. The economy was healthy because the state had so many different businesses.

Did You Know?

On May 18, 1980, something happened that rarely occurs in the United States: a volcano erupted. Mount St. Helens, a volcano in southwestern Washington, exploded.

It had been dormant since 1857. In March of 1980, steam shot out of the top. Cracks in the side of the mountain began to appear.

On the morning of May 18, an earthquake created a landslide, and then the top of the mountain exploded. Lava and mud flowed down the mountain. Gas and ash went 16 miles (26 km) high. Ash and other particles fell

A forest of blown down trees are covered in volcanic ash.

as far away as western Minnesota. So much ash fell in Spokane, 250 miles (402 km) away, that the sun was blocked out. Trees and vegetation were knocked down for 200 square miles (518 sq km).

Sadly, 57 people were killed. The eruption of Mount St. Helens was one of the biggest explosions ever in North America.

People

Seattle (1786–1866) was a chief of the Suquamish and Duwamish Native American tribes. He was born on Blake Island on Puget Sound. When white settlers were stealing Indian land, he didn't want warfare. He tried to keep the peace between the settlers and the Native American tribes. The city of Seattle is named after him. He is buried on the Suquamish reservation in Port Madison.

Bill Gates (1955-) was born in Seattle. He began writing computer software when he was 13 years old. After he left Harvard University, he began Microsoft Corporation. The company provided software for personal computers. He soon became one of the richest men in the world. More recently, Gates has spent most of his time working on a foundation he started, which gives money to needy projects.

Actress **Hilary Swank** (1974-) was born in Lincoln, Nebraska, but moved to Bellingham, Washington, when she was young. She got her first big Hollywood role in 1994, in the movie *The Next Karate Kid*. She has won two Academy Awards, for her movies *Boys Don't Cry* and *Million Dollar Baby*. The Academy Award is the highest honor in Hollywood.

Bing Crosby (1903-1977) was born in Tacoma, Washington. He became one of the most popular singers and actors in history. His biggest hit song was "White Christmas." Crosby also starred in many movies, both comedies and dramas. He won an Academy Award for his role as a priest in the 1944 movie *Going My Way*.

Chester Carlson (1906–1968) was born in Seattle, Washington. He invented the machine that could photocopy other documents. He called the process electrophotography.

In 1944, he sold the idea to a company that became Xerox Corporation. They made the machine and sold it to businesses. It changed the way companies worked. The invention also made other machines possible, such as laser printers.

Cities

Seattle is in the northwest corner of the United States. The population of Seattle and its surrounding cities is more than 3.6 million. Seattle was named after the Native American Chief Seattle, chief of the Duwamish and Suquamish tribes. Today, many large companies operate or have their headquarters in the Seattle area, including Boeing, Starbucks Coffee, and Amazon.com. The city is also home to the University of Washington, which was founded in 1861.

Tacoma is on the south end of Puget Sound. Its population is 196,520. The area was originally inhabited by the Puyallup Indians. European settlers began to move in to the area in the 1850s and 1860s. It was incorporated in 1875. Today, it is an important manufacturing and shipping center.

Olympia is the state capital of Washington. It is about 25 miles (40 km) southwest of the city of Tacoma. Olympia's population is 44,925. The city began in the 1840s. It is called Olympia because the Olympic Mountains are in the distance. The Evergreen State College is located in Olympia.

Spokane is on the eastern edge of Washington, just a few miles from the Idaho border. Its population is 200,975. It is named after the Spokane Native

American tribe. The city is home to several colleges, including Eastern Washington University, Gonzaga University, and Washington State University-Spokane.

Vancouver is on the north bank of the Columbia River, across from Portland, Oregon. It is named after English explorer George Vancouver, who visited the area in 1792. With a population of 161,436, Vancouver has become a center for technology and service businesses.

Transportation

There are two main interstate highways that go across Washington. Interstate I-90 goes east and west, through Spokane and Seattle. Interstate I-5 goes north and south. It goes from Vancouver, Washington, through Tacoma and Seattle, north toward Canada.

There are 11 primary commercial airports in Washington. The largest is Seattle-Tacoma International Airport. It serves more than 30 million passengers a year. It is the 18th-busiest airport in the United States. There are more than 140 other airports in the state.

Downtown Seattle and Elliot Bay are seen over the wing of a jet as it circles to land in Seattle.

The Washington State Department of Transportation runs a fleet of ferries. A ferry is a boat that takes people and often cars across a waterway. The Washington State Ferries operate between the communities that border Puget Sound. The ferry system is one of the largest in the world.

Ferries take people and cars across Washington's many waterways.

Natural Resources

A logging truck.

Washington has many natural resources that provide jobs and help the state.

Washington's huge forests provide lumber. The forests also provide homes for many different kinds of wildlife.

The ocean along the west coast of Washington is a prime fishing area. Commercial fisheries catch salmon, halibut, cod, herring, and shellfish.

Water in the big rivers, like the Columbia River, make good fishing for trout and other fish. The water also provides for irrigation to water farms.

Farmers in Washington grow many crops. Winter wheat is an important crop. Farmers also grow barley, peas, and lentils. Potatoes and other vegetables are also grown on Washington farms. Some farmers raise chicken and turkeys.

Washington has orchards full of apples. Washington farmers grow more apples than any other state.

Washington apples are enjoyed by people around the world. Thousands of bushels of apples are grown in the state every year.

Industry

A Boeing 747 plane is built in Everett, Washington.

Washington has many kinds of businesses. These businesses give people jobs and help the economy.

One of Washington's big industries is manufacturing. Airplanes are built in Washington. The United States Navy builds ships and submarines.

Tourism is another important industry. With three national parks, a long ocean coastline, mountains, and forests, many people come to enjoy the outdoors.

Agriculture, including dairy and cattle farming, is an important industry. Financial institutions and computer technology form an important part of the economy. Oil refineries take Alaskan oil and turn it into gasoline. Many films and TV commercials are shot in Washington.

One of the largest power plants in the United States is in Washington. It is a hydroelectric plant at the Grand Coulee Dam on the Columbia River. Hydroelectric power is clean because it uses water to generate electricity.

The Columbia River flows through a narrow channel, tamed by the Grand Coulee Dam. The construction of the dam has been called the Eighth Wonder of the World.

Sports

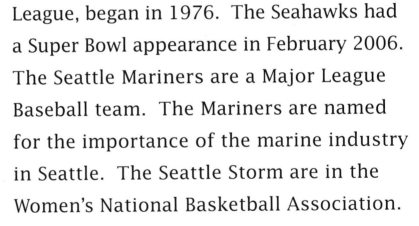

Washington has several professional sports teams. The Seattle Seahawks, a team in the National Football League, began in 1976. The Seahawks had a Super Bowl appearance in February 2006. The Seattle Mariners are a Major League Baseball team. The Mariners are named for the importance of the marine industry in Seattle. The Seattle Storm are in the Women's National Basketball Association. The team won the WNBA Championship in 2004.

Soccer, hockey, rugby, and mixed martial arts sports teams also make Seattle their home.

There are many things to do in Washington for people who love the outdoors. There are mountains to climb and ski. Hunters and hikers like the dense forests. Campers love the lakes and streams. There are great fishing opportunities on the coast and on the lakes of Washington.

A skier enjoys the slopes of Washington's Cascade Mountains.

Entertainment

Washington has many art galleries, museums, and art and theater groups.

There are more than 25 major art galleries in the state, and many smaller ones. Many of the museums feature arts and crafts from the Native American people who lived in the area.

In 1962, Seattle hosted the World's Fair. The city built the Space Needle, a very high tower with a restaurant on top. It is 605 feet (184 m) high. When it was built in 1962, it was the highest building west of the Mississippi River.

Space Needle

The Seattle Symphony, formed in 1903, is nationally known. Seattle also has operas and theater companies. Seattle's Woodland Park Zoo began in 1887. It now is home to more than 1,000 animals.

Timeline

10,000-15,000 Years Ago—Ancestors of the Native Americans arrive in the area of present-day Washington.

1579—English explorer Sir Francis Drake sails along the Washington coast.

1775—Spanish Explorer Bruno de Heceta maps the Washington coast.

1792—Englishman Captain James Cook explores the coast and waterways.

1805—The Lewis and Clark Expedition reaches the Washington area.

1825—Hudson's Bay Company establishes Fort Vancouver.

1843—American settlers in Oregon Territory set up a temporary government.

1853—Washington Territory is organized, the same size as the current state of Washington.

1889—Washington becomes the 42nd state.

1929—The Great Depression begins, hitting Washington hard.

1941-1945—America's involvement in World War II brings better economic times to the state.

1980—Mount St. Helens erupts on the morning of May 18th, killing 57 people and thousands of plants and animals.

2004—The Seattle Storm wins the Women's National Basketball Association Championship.

Glossary

Chinook—A Native American tribe.

Coulee—A deep dry valley, cut by runoff from a melting glacier.

Glacier—A large body of ice, formed from melting and refreezing snow, that can slowly spread outward or retreat.

Great Depression—A time of worldwide economic hardship beginning in 1929. Many people lost their jobs and had little money. The Great Depression finally eased in the mid-1930s, but didn't end until many countries entered World War II, around 1939.

Hydroelectric Power—A renewable energy source. Flowing water, rather than oil or coal, is used to generate electricity.

Lewis and Clark Expedition—An exploration of the American West, led by Meriwether Lewis and William Clark, from 1804-1806.

Nez Percé—A Native American tribe.

Pelts—The skins of animals. People in the 1700s and 1800s paid a lot for pelts of certain animals, like the sea otter.

Plateau—A large flat area that is lifted up from the surrounding area.

Sound—A waterway or ocean inlet.

Suquamish—A Native American tribe.

World War I—A war that was fought in Europe from 1914 to 1918, involving countries around the world. The United States entered the war in April 1917.

World War II—A conflict across the world, lasting from 1939-1945. The United States entered the war in December of 1941.

Index